Mickey the Sheep Dog

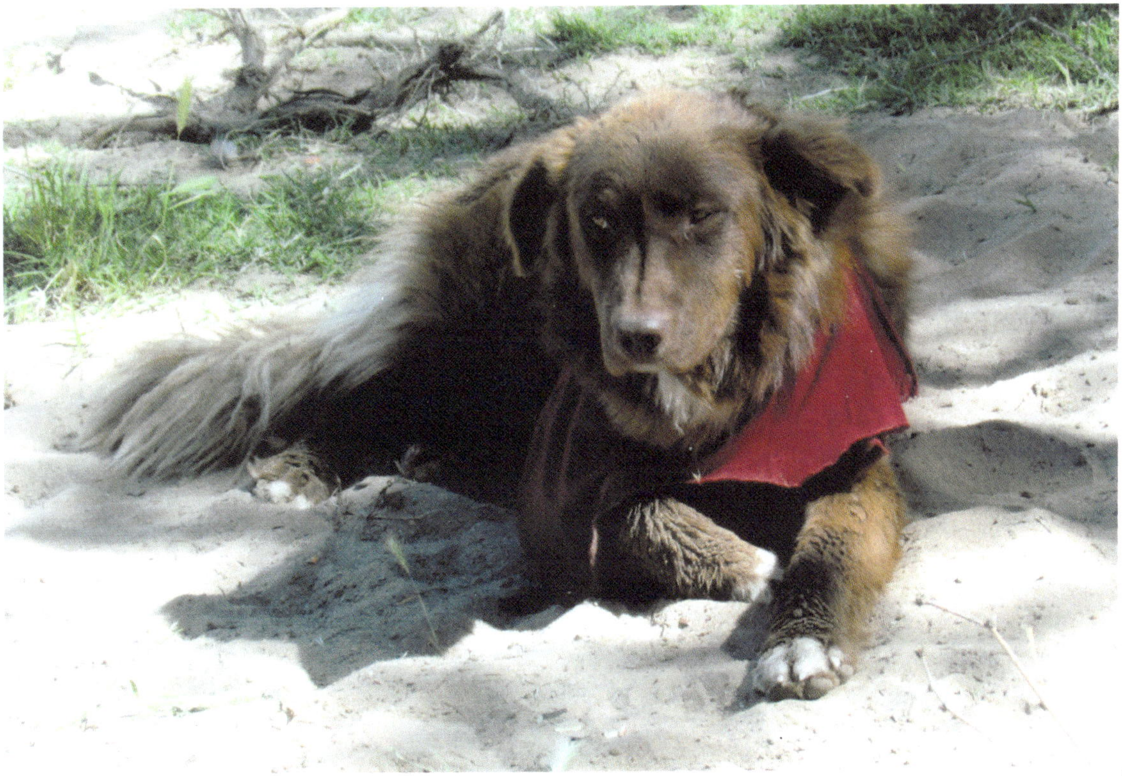

Cindy Shanks

"Paws" to Read! Cindy Shanks

AuthorHouse™
1663 Liberty Drive
Bloomington, IN 47403
www.authorhouse.com
Phone: 1-800-839-8640

© 2011 Cindy Shanks. All Rights Reserved.

No part of this book may be reproduced, stored in a retrieval system,
or transmitted by any means without the written permission of the author.

First published by AuthorHouse 10/19/2011

ISBN: 978-1-4670-6237-4 (sc)

Library of Congress Control Number: 2011918398

Printed in the United States of America

This book is printed on acid-free paper.

Because of the dynamic nature of the Internet, any web addresses or links contained in this book may have changed since publication and may no longer be valid. The views expressed in this work are solely those of the author and do not necessarily reflect the views of the publisher, and the publisher hereby disclaims any responsibility for them.

My name is Mickey and I am a Border Collie. My whole family works with the Dobson sheep on the Heber-Reno Sheep Trail. In the winter, we live on a farm near Florence, Arizona where the ewes give birth to their lambs. In the spring, we herd the sheep to the White Mountains for the summer.

The trail up into the mountains is 220 miles long and it takes us 45-50 days to reach the cool summer pastures near Greer. There are 2000 sheep in each band and there are two bands that still walk this old, historic trail. Our job is to help the herders keep the sheep safe and on the trail. In August, we walk the same trail out of the mountains, back to the farm.

I am the youngest dog in my family. My mom, my dad and my three big brothers also work with the sheep. We walk with the sheep on the trail, but we also herd them in the fields of Northern Arizona in the summer. I love my job, and I am trying hard to learn from my family how to be a great sheep dog.

My mom's name is Chispa and she is a black and white Border Collie. She is not walking the trail or working with the sheep this year because she is going to have puppies soon. This summer, mom and her friend Sally are living at Felipe's house at the ranch. Felipe is the foreman for the Dobson sheep and we belong to him.

Border Collies have very special traits that make us excellent herding dogs. My mom's special trait is her desire to please her herder. She loves to be with people and will work very hard to make sure she does what the herders ask her to do. I must be like my mom because I love to be with people too. It makes me very happy when the herders tell me I have done a good job.

My dad's name is Champ. He is a very hardworking sheepdog. He does not like to be with people, he just likes to work hard and do what his herder asks him to do. He likes to work with Diercio or Hugo.

His special trait is that he is very, very smart. He knows what he should do even before he is told. He watches the sheep and is ready when his herder tells him to go. I hope I grow up to be as smart as my dad.

I have a brother named Chochie who likes to work with dad. He looks like dad too, except he has a very short tail. Chochie works very hard, but his special traits are that he is very calm and very fast. He never nips at the sheep or barks at them. He is patient but firm.

Last year, the herders tried to separate dad and Chochie on the trail. Chochie didn't like that at all, so he left his herd and went very fast over many miles to catch up with dad's herd and walk with him. Now they stay together on the trail and they are both happy.

My brother Duke is the same age as Chochie, but he is black and white like mom. He is very shy and doesn't like to be around anyone but Chagua, his herder. He watches Chagua all the time and knows exactly what he is expected to do.

Duke has the Border Collie stare, the "eye", which makes the sheep do exactly what he wants. He always keeps them under control. He often uses his stare on other animals, and it works there too. He has a typical Border Collie working style. His head is low to the ground, his hindquarters are high, and his tail is often tucked between his legs.

My favorite brother is named Azul, which is the Spanish word for blue. He has one brown eye and one blue eye. He loves to be around people, but he always watches his herder and is ready to work.

Azul has a great smile. He shows all of his teeth. It looks a little scary, but he just wants to be your friend. Azul likes to work with all of the herders, but he is working with Richard this summer. Richard is in charge of a large herd of ewes and their lambs that were born in the spring. They came to the mountains in trucks because the lambs were too young to walk the trail.

Azul has all of the best traits of a good sheep dog. He likes to be with people and please them, just like mom. He is also very smart, just like dad. He works fast like Chochie and never nips at the sheep. And, he is learning to use the "eye" stare like Duke. Azul is just a year older than me and he is growing out of being a puppy and becoming a grownup dog.

Border Collies grow up very slowly. I am still in the puppy stage that may last 2-3 years. Sometimes I get very excited and I don't pay attention to Diercio and my job. I still have a lot to learn about being a good sheep dog.

Each of the herders has a different way of giving us commands. Some of the herders use hand movements to show us where they want us to go. They may also use voice commands if they know that we understand them.

Some of the herders whistle to let us know what to do. The whistles may sound slightly different for each command. We like to stay with the same herder because we learn their whistles and can do our job well.

There is another dog on the trail with us. He is a white Pyrenees. His name is Blue because he has a blue collar. Blue is not a herding dog. He is a guardian dog and he protects the sheep by living with them all the time and keeping predators away. He keeps away dangerous animals because he is very big and he has a loud, scary bark.

Mark and Candi, who manage the Dobson sheep, have a Pyrenees named Isabella. She has 8 new, white puppies. They will meet the sheep when they are very young so they can learn to work as guardian dogs and protect the sheep, just like Blue.

The hardest part of our job is working on the trail. In the spring, we start walking in the desert near Mesa, Arizona. The desert can be very dangerous. Last year, a rattlesnake bit my mom on the face. She was really sick for a while, but she is ok now.

We have to be careful of the cactus too. Diercio sometimes gives us a haircut so we don't catch all the stickers as we walk. We look funny, but we are much cooler and the cactus needles don't stick to our hair.

Along the trail, we get hot and dusty. Sometimes we cool off by jumping into the sheeps' water tanks, or into a pond or creek. It just feels good.

There are a lot of places along the trail where there is no water, so we just take a good dust bath to get rid of bugs and stickers and cactus needles. It feels so good to scratch and roll around in the dirt.

We always remember that our job is to herd the sheep. Sometimes it is through the hot, dusty desert, sometimes in the northern grasslands and sometimes in the tall trees of Northern Arizona. We are always working.

We move the sheep across busy highways and down dusty country roads. We run to the right and left of the herd to make sure they stay on the trail straight ahead. Last year, Dad and Chochie had to get in front of the sheep at Bushnell Tanks. They had to turn them around and move them back down the hill into the pasture for siesta.

When we get to the summer pastures in June, we still have a job to do. At the end of the spring trail, we round up the sheep and herd them into the corrals to be sheared. Azul really tries to help Richard, but there isn't much for him to do.

Duke's job is to help Chagua move the burros across the highway and into the field. He makes sure the burros get inside the fence and don't wander around near the cars. The burros carry the packs on the trail. Then they spend the summer grazing in the national forest.

When the burros have been moved to their grazing land and the sheep have been sheared, my family and I join our herders. Our job for the summer is to help the herders keep the sheep together as they move around the green meadows and thick forests of the White Mountains.

We all like summertime the best. We live near our herders' trailers. We enjoy the cool temperatures, the thick, green grass, the beautiful wildflowers and the freedom of the open land. Summer in the mountains is good for dogs.

We are working sheep dogs. Our job is to herd the sheep through fields, around fences or gates, and into corrals or fenced areas. There are other Border Collies who are trained by their handlers to do all of the same jobs, but in a contest. These contests are sheep dog trials.

This is Cait. She is a 4 year old Border Collie who lives with her handler Carie in California. Carie has taught Cait all of the skills that she needs to compete in sheep dog trials. Cait is still young and is only in trials near her home. As she gets older and begins winning contests, she will move up from pro-novice level competition to open trials all over the country.

Carie gives Cait directions using a special whistle. This is Carie's whistle made from buffalo horn. She also uses voice commands and hand signals. Cait listens and watches very closely to make sure she does what Carie asks her to do.

Some of the commands for the sheep dogs trials are:
  Come by – tells the dog to go left
  Way to me – go right
  Come here or here to me – come to the handler
  Down or lie down – stops the dog
  Walk up – moves the dog straight toward the sheep
  Get out or get back out – move away from the sheep
  Take time – slow down
  Look back – dog goes to gather more sheep
  That'll do – orders the dog to quit working
There is also a special whistle sound for each of these commands.

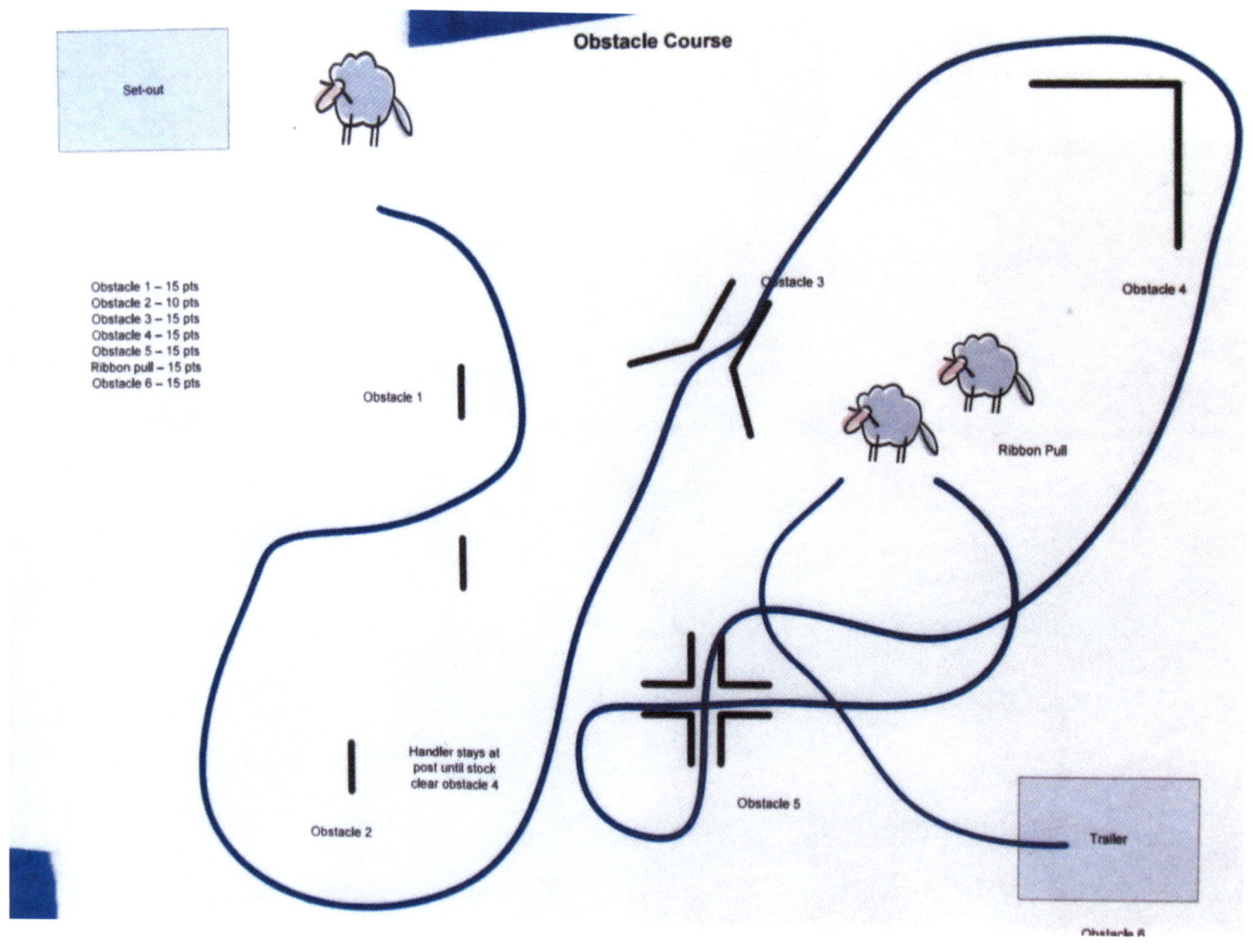

There are many different ways to set up the field for sheep dog trials. The course always includes work in the outfield. This is where the dog shows that he can find the sheep, get control of them and move them calmly and quietly to the handler. The handler must stand at a post and only give directions verbally, or with a whistle.

The dog brings the sheep to the handler, moves them around the post and away from the handler. The sheep are then herded through sets of gates and into a large circle. The handler moves into the circle to shed, or separate, the sheep into two groups. The dog then moves one group into a pen or truck. The dog and the handler have to work very closely to complete this job.

There is a time limit for all of these activities to be completed. There are total points set for the whole course and points are taken away for each mistake. The winner of the trials is the team, a dog and handler, with the most points.

At the end of a run, Cait is very hot and tired and goes straight to a water tank to drink and cool off. All of the handlers love their dogs and give them lots of care and attention for working hard.

The Border Collies in the trials and dogs working with sheep on a ranch have the same traits. We all learn to understand sheep and control them. We are strong and can work hard for a long time. We are very smart and concentrate on the job. But the best trait of all is our love for people. We love our herders and handlers and they love us too.

Acknowledgements

My first thank you goes to the Dobson family for allowing me to photograph all aspects of the sheep trail, and the day-to-day life of sheep ranching. I want to say a big thank you to Felipe and the herders for allowing me to follow them around and photograph them these last three years. It has been a life-changing experience. I want to thank Fred and Steve for their editing expertise, good humor and patience.

Thank you to Carie and Cait for allowing me to share my photographs of their competition at the sheep dog trials. Thanks to Carie for answering my endless questions. Cait, you are on your way to becoming a champion.

If you want to learn more about the historic Heber-Reno Sheep Trail, contact Authorhouse to purchase <u>Emily Walks the Sheep Trail</u>. This story is told by a young lamb experiencing the trail with her mother. In <u>Alfonso Grows Up on the Sheep Trail</u>, a young burro makes friends and learns to work as a pack burro on the trail.

CPSIA information can be obtained
at www.ICGtesting.com
Printed in the USA
260992LV00001B